SETTING THE RECORD STRAIGHT
MORMONS & SCIENCE

Cover: The two symbols on the cover represent the two themes of this book. The Prophet Joseph Smith was central to the restoration of the ancient gospel of Jesus Christ and represents revelation of truth from God to humankind in our day. The double helix of DNA that contains the hereditary information in living things symbolizes the reach of modern scientific achievement.

SETTING THE RECORD STRAIGHT
MORMONS & SCIENCE

Rodney J. Brown, Ph.D.

Millennial Press, Inc.
P.O. Box 1741
Orem, UT 84059

ISBN: 1-932597-45-X

Copyright © 2008 Millennial Press

All rights reserved. Reproduction in whole or any parts thereof in any form or by any media without written permission is prohibited. The only exception to this would be the use of brief passages for critical review and analysis. This work is not an official publication of The Church of Jesus Christ of Latter-day Saints. The views expressed herein are the responsibility of the author and do not necessarily represent the position of the Church or of Millennial Press, Inc. Scientists who are members of The Church of Jesus Christ of Latter-day Saints do not agree on every topic covered in this book.

Cover design and typesetting by Adam Riggs

Dedication

To my wife and sweetheart, Sandra Brown, whose thoughts and influence are scattered throughout this book.

Contents

Introduction: Balancing Science with Religion 1
Questions and Answers 15
Appendix I—Some Abandoned Scientific Theories 43
Appendix II—Origin of Man Packet 47
Endnotes 61
Bibliography 65
Author Biographical Information 69

Introduction: Balancing Science with Religion

One of the many remarkable characteristics of humankind is our desire to understand our surroundings and ourselves. We are curious. We want to know what the universe is and how it works. We want to know where it came from and when and how. Most absorbing of all is our desire to know who we are—our origin and the purpose of our existence.[1] Fortunately for us, we are endowed not only with the desire to know these things but also with the abilities necessary to discover much of what we want to know.

Most people look to science or religion for explanations. Though the main interests of science and religion differ, many important topics attract the attention of both. However, religions often disagree among themselves, and scientists disagree with each other. We, of course, also hear of differences of opinion between science and religion.

How, then, can members of The Church of Jesus Christ of Latter-day Saints (Mormons) balance science with their religion? That is the topic of this book.

Truth

We can begin by recognizing that facts do not change. A correct answer exists for every question we could ask. We sometimes refer to eternal truths in a religious context, but eternal truths are not limited to topics generally recognized as belonging to religion. These truths are facts that are what they are and will not change. They are things as they really happened regardless of how we think they happened—things as they really are regardless of how we think they are. They do not change over time, with changing circumstances, or in any other way. They are not affected by popularity or lack of popularity. They are reality.

> "And truth is knowledge of things as they are, and as they were, and as they are to come" (D&C 93:24).

President Brigham Young said, "...truth is calculated to sustain itself; it is based upon eternal facts and will endure, while all else will, sooner or later, perish."[2]

It is easy to convince ourselves that what we think to be true matches this definition of truth. However, no matter how carefully we try to get it right, our personal versions of what is true contain mistruths, half-truths, untruths, and so forth. Things we have thought true for a long time are hard to discard, even when they are shown to be untrue.[3] To find real truth requires a level of humility that is difficult for us to achieve.

The Creator

Another foundation principle that we can rely on is the knowledge that God is omniscient, that He knows everything. The unchangeable facts that are the ultimate answers to all our questions are known to God.

> "...all things are present with me, for I know them all" (Moses 1:6).

> "Known unto God are all his works from the beginning of the world" (Acts 15:18).

This gives us not only a solid foundation, but also a clear perspective. The more we can look at things the way God looks at them, the better our chances are of understanding what we see.

Joseph Smith said, "The heavens declare the glory of God, and the firmament showeth His handiwork; and a moment's reflection is sufficient to teach every man of common intelligence, that all these are not the mere productions of chance, nor could they be supported by any power less than an Almighty hand."[4]

The following verses remind us that we have only a minute portion of the knowledge of God's creations.

> "And worlds without number have I created; and I also created them for mine own purpose; and by my Son I created them, which is mine Only Begotten.
>
> "But only an account of this earth, and the inhabitants thereof, give I unto you. For behold, there are many worlds that have passed away by the word of my power. And there are many that now stand, and innumerable are they unto man; but all things are numbered unto me, for they are mine and I know them" (Moses 1:33, 35).

We are also told in these verses that God's many creations were for His purposes (that we only vaguely understand) and that His Only Begotten Son created them. Humility concerning our position, wonder at the magnitude of God's creations, and awareness of the central role of Jesus Christ in all creation are essential if we are to stand on solid footing as we search for truth.

Effort

We might ask, "Since God knows everything, why does He not pass all this knowledge on to His children?" God could easily tell us everything we want to know and much more. Instead, He helps us learn gradually, just as we do when we try to help our children learn what we know.

"For precept must be upon precept, precept upon precept; line upon line, line upon line; here a little, and there a little" (Isaiah 28:10).

There is an order to acquiring knowledge that cannot be ignored. Arithmetic comes before algebra, algebra comes before calculus, and so on. Spiritual knowledge also has faith and obedience prerequisites.

Learning is most effective when responsibility rests more on the learner than on the teacher. Finding things out for ourselves works better than being given the answers.

> "But, behold, I say unto you, that you must study it out in your mind; then you must ask me if it be right, and if it is right I will cause that your bosom shall burn within you; therefore, you shall feel that it is right" (D&C 9:8).

If we are to understand life and the universe in which we live, we have to work hard, using every method available to us to find the truth.

The Scope of Mormonism

The restored gospel makes it easy to balance the theories of science with religious faith. President Young explained the relationship of revealed religion and science this way:

> "If you can find a truth in heaven, earth or hell, it belongs to our doctrine. We believe it; it is ours; we claim it....
>
> "Our religion is simply the truth. It is all said in this one expression—it embraces all truth, wherever found, in all the works of God and man that are visible or invisible to mortal eye....
>
> "'Mormonism,' so-called, embraces every principle pertaining to life and salvation, for time and eternity. No matter who has it. If the infidel has got truth it belongs to 'Mormonism.' The truth and sound doctrine

INTRODUCTION: BALANCING SCIENCE WITH RELIGION — 5

> possessed by the sectarian world, and they have a great deal, all belong to this Church. . . . 'Mormonism' includes all truth. . . .
>
> "It embraces every fact in the heavens and in the heaven of heavens—every fact there is upon the surface of the earth, in the bowels of the earth, and in the starry heavens; in fine, it embraces all truth there is in all the eternities of the Gods."[5]

He said also, "In these respects we differ from the Christian world, for our religion will not clash with or contradict the facts of science in any particular."[6]

In responding to a request to speak on our leading doctrines, President John Taylor began by saying:

> "In regard to our religion, I will say that it embraces every principle of truth and intelligence pertaining to us as moral, intellectual, mortal and immortal beings, pertaining to this world and the world that is to come. We are open to truth of every kind, no matter whence it comes, where it originates, or who believes in it. Truth, when preceded by the little word 'all,' comprises everything that has ever existed or that ever will exist and be known by and among men in time and through the endless ages of eternity; and it is the duty of all intelligent beings who are responsible and amenable to God for their acts, to search after truth, and to permit it to influence them and their acts and general course in life, independent of all bias or pre-conceived notions, however specious and plausible they may be."[7]

To members of The Church of Jesus Christ of Latter-day Saints, the search for truth and understanding is a wide-open field. It goes beyond simple curiosity. Our desire to emulate God motivates us to understand Him and all his creations.

The Search for Truth

Since its beginning, the LDS Church has put a premium on knowledge and learning. Our scriptures point out both the importance of knowledge and the necessity of obtaining it by both spiritual and secular means.

> "The glory of God is intelligence, or, in other words, light and truth.
>
> "Light and truth forsake that evil one. . . .
>
> "But I have commanded you to bring up your children in light and truth" (D&C 93:36–37, 40).
>
> "Whatever principle of intelligence we attain unto in this life, it will rise with us in the resurrection.
>
> "And if a person gains more knowledge and intelligence in this life through his diligence and obedience than another, he will have so much the advantage in the world to come" (D&C 130:18).
>
> "Teach ye diligently and my grace shall attend you, that you may be instructed more perfectly in theory, in principle, in doctrine, in the law of the gospel, in all things that pertain unto the kingdom of God, that are expedient for you to understand;
>
> "Of things both in heaven and in the earth, and under the earth; things which have been, things which are, things which must shortly come to pass; things which are at home, things which are abroad; the wars and the perplexities of the nations, and the judgments which are on the land; and a knowledge also of countries and of kingdoms" (D&C 88:78–79).

These and other scriptures point out the importance of both religious learning and secular learning. Many branches of secular learning are beyond the scope of this book. Here we are looking only at the approaches of science and religion to finding truth.

As we approach truth through both science and religion, some feel caught in an uncomfortable void between faith in science and religious faith. This leads some to think that they must abandon either science or religion to deal with apparent conflicts. Elder Boyd K. Packer has pointed out the necessity of balance:

> "Each of us must accommodate the mixture of reason and revelation in our lives. The gospel not only permits but requires it. An individual who concentrates on either side solely and alone will lose both balance and perspective."[8]

As we learn more, as we approach the truth from both directions, the apparent void will disappear. The destination is the same, independent of the route taken to get there. When science and religion arrive at the truth, they are at the same place and in perfect agreement with each other.

We cannot immediately know everything we would like to know. There is much that we will never know in our lifetimes. Even partial answers can be frustrating. This presents the temptation to jump for simple, easy explanations of things that cannot be simply or easily explained. The world in which we live is not black and white. It is full of color and is sometimes a bit blurry. It is much clearer and more beautiful if we humbly and patiently try to fit together all the pieces available from all the possible sources.

Religion

Religion approaches an understanding of life and the universe by asking, "Why?" Though interested in how, where, when, and related questions, religion's greater curiosity is purpose. From a religious point of view, why things are as they are is more important than how they came to be that way.[9]

The source of information in religion is revelation. Answers are not found by trial and error, speculation, and so forth; rather, they are found only by communication from God. God, not man, decides what to reveal and when and to whom to reveal it. Information received by revelation has the solid attribute of being true.

The ability to separate revealed truth from less-reliable information is given to everyone. Christ said, "If any man will do his will, he shall know of the doctrine, whether it be of God, or whether I speak of myself" (John 7:17).

This is a formula for both recognizing truth and detecting untruth. Elder Bruce R. McConkie described this process as personal revelation:

> "Would you like a formula to tell you how to get personal revelation? It might be written in many ways. My formula is simply this:
> "1. Search the Scriptures.
> "2. Keep the Commandments.
> "3. Ask in Faith.
> "Any person who will do this will get his heart so in tune with the Infinite that there will come into his being, from the 'still small voice,' the eternal realities of religion. And as he progresses and advances and comes nearer to God, there will be a day when he will entertain angels, when he will see visions, and the final end is to view the face of God."[10]

Alma, in the Book of Mormon, gave an example of the same process:

> "Now, as I said concerning faith—that it was not a perfect knowledge—even so it is with my words. Ye cannot know of their surety at first, unto perfection, any more than faith is a perfect knowledge.
> "But behold, if ye will awake and arouse your faculties, even to an experiment upon my words, and exercise a particle of faith, yea, even if ye can no more than de-

INTRODUCTION: BALANCING SCIENCE WITH RELIGION — 9

sire to believe, let this desire work in you, even until ye believe in a manner that ye can give place for a portion of my words.

"Now, we will compare the word unto a seed. Now, if ye give place, that a seed may be planted in your heart, behold, if it be a true seed, or a good seed, if ye do not cast it out by your unbelief, that ye will resist the Spirit of the Lord, behold, it will begin to swell within your breasts; and when you feel these swelling motions, ye will begin to say within yourselves—It must needs be that this is a good seed, or that the word is good, for it beginneth to enlarge my soul; yea, it beginneth to enlighten my understanding, yea, it beginneth to be delicious to me.

"Now behold, would not this increase your faith? I say unto you, Yea; nevertheless it hath not grown up to a perfect knowledge.

"But behold, as the seed swelleth, and sprouteth, and beginneth to grow, then you must needs say that the seed is good; for behold it swelleth, and sprouteth, and beginneth to grow. And now, behold, will not this strengthen your faith? Yea, it will strengthen your faith: for ye will say I know that this is a good seed; for behold it sprouteth and beginneth to grow.

"And now, behold, are ye sure that this is a good seed? I say unto you, Yea; for every seed bringeth forth unto its own likeness.

"Therefore, if a seed groweth it is good, but if it groweth not, behold it is not good, therefore it is cast away.

"And now, behold, because ye have tried the experiment, and planted the seed, and it swelleth and sprouteth, and beginneth to grow, ye must needs know that the seed is good.

"And now, behold, is your knowledge perfect? Yea, your knowledge is perfect in that thing, and your faith is dormant; and this because you know, for ye know that the word hath swelled your souls, and ye also know that it hath sprouted up, that your understanding doth begin to be enlightened, and your mind doth begin to expand" (Alma 32:26–34).

The kind of experiment described here is different from a scientific experiment. Spiritual experiments are designed to discover the truth of something, while scientific experiments are designed to disprove things. This will be explained more fully in a discussion of the scientific method.

Because much remains unrevealed and humankind has an insatiable desire to know things, some unnecessary problems arise. Revealed information can be endlessly reformulated and elaborated. Such activities do not uncover additional truth, but they can generate misinformation. Hence, on many topics we hear arguments credited to God that are extrapolated beyond what He has revealed.

Science

Science explains life and the universe based on a different method of discovery. It has little interest in why things are as they are; rather, it is interested in how they are and how they came to be that way.[11]

Our understanding of how science works has matured over time. What was called science long ago only vaguely resembled today's science. The great philosophers —Socrates, Plato, and others—employed a simple way of discovering knowledge. They thought about things and came to conclusions. The idea was that the mind could deduce truths on its own.[12] This method, called rationalism, led to some valuable insights but has some serious weaknesses when used to describe the physical world. Thinking about whether the earth is flat or round will never get to the answer unless someone looks at the earth.

Endless discussions and arguments intent on persuasion more than on discovery eventually led people to do what seems obvious to us today: look for evidence. At the urging of Robert Hooke, experience was proposed as being critical to the discovery of truth.[13] It then became popular to make large numbers of observations from which conclusions could be deduced. This came to be called *empiricism,* based on the use of empirical evidence. Valuable discoveries were made using this method, and observation was established as the core of scientific research. Isaac Newton was one of the early adopters of this new experimental philosophy. By the way, Newton openly discussed God in his great treatise on gravity and the laws of motion, *Principia Mathematica.*

Albert Einstein's new ideas challenged those of Newton and proved them wrong in some respects during a time when a new view of how science works was emerging. Karl Popper became the spokesman for *critical rationalism.*[14] The main idea of this view is that theories can be proven false or not proven false, but they can never be proven to be true. This realization has propelled the great surge of scientific progress in the past one hundred years.

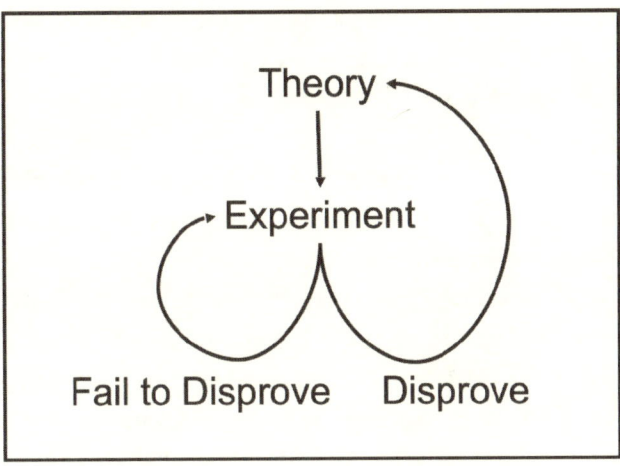

Figure 1. The Scientific Method

The method used by science to find truth is appropriately called the *scientific method* (Figure 1).[15] It is based on observations and follows Popper's premise that a thing cannot be proven to be true, but can be proven not to be true. Here is how it works:

1. A theory that seems to explain all that has been observed is developed.
2. An experiment is designed to test the theory—to try to prove the theory wrong.
3. The experiment is conducted.
4. If the experiment is unable to prove the theory wrong, more experiments are designed and conducted, always trying to disprove the theory.
5. If an experiment succeeds in disproving the theory, a new theory is developed, and the process begins again.

This method exposes much that is not true by slowly eliminating theories and thus causing them to be refined. It brings us incrementally closer to the truth but never quite to it. Some theories are quickly discredited; others survive much longer. A hierarchy of theories develops, with those that have withstood challenges for the longest time as the foundation of the pile, and the newer, less-tested ones are exposed on the surface. All are theories that have not been proven wrong rather than facts that have been proven true. Appendix 1 describes some theories that have been proven wrong or partially wrong after being generally accepted for a long time.

Several opportunities to misuse the scientific method present themselves. Most of these are the result of forgetting or ignoring the basis of the method. For example, it is common to speak of scientific theories as facts. To continue making progress in scientific discovery, we must remember that the whole compilation of scientific knowledge is based on theories that continue to be tested.

Practicing scientists can easily fall into error by forgetting that experiments are to disprove theories, not to prove them. It is relatively easy to design experiments that fail to disprove a theory. It is a grave error to accept such failure as proof that the theory is true. This pitfall is particularly tempting to those testing theories they hope are true. The result of this approach is a return to the pre-sixteenth century way of trying to explain the universe.

Another challenge is the limited scope of our ability to observe. We have access to only a small percentage of the spectrum. There is a limit beyond which, even with the best instruments, things are too small to see. As we look into the sky, because of the time light takes to travel, we see what far away objects looked like in the past. We can see the present only of things close to us. This makes it particularly difficult to formulate theories based on observations. Experimental science does very well considering the view we have through our small window. If we could see more, our theories would be better and science would make faster progress.

Some theories are harder to test and therefore inherently more difficult to disprove, even if they are not true. Devising tests for theories that are impossible to observe with our physical senses requires great ingenuity. Such difficult theories often require us to use evidence left from the past rather than doing controlled experiments.

Summary

People have an innate urge to know how and why the world and the universe came to be as they are. God knows the unchangeable truths that are the answers to our questions. We have only a minute portion of the knowledge of what He, through His Only Begotten Son, has created for His own purposes. Humility is invaluable as we strive to learn and discover all we can.

To members of The Church of Jesus Christ of Latter-day Saints, the search for truth and understanding is a wide-open field. Mormonism embraces all truth, whatever the source or the method used to find it. The answers to many of our questions are still in the void between faith in science and religious faith. However, as we approach the truth the apparent void will disappear. When science and religion both arrive at the truth, they will be in perfect agreement with each other.

Science and religion contribute in different ways and thereby complement each other. Religion is most interested in, and is most helpful in, understanding why we and everything else exist. The only source of truth in religion is revelation. Science is more interested in, and is more helpful in, discovering how things work. The scientific method brings us gradually closer to the truth—not by proving things true but by exposing ideas that are not true.

We cannot immediately know everything we would like to know. Even partial answers can be frustrating. This presents the temptation to jump for simple, easy explanations of things that cannot be simply or easily explained. However, the world in which we live is not black and white. It is full of color. Our view of it is much clearer and more beautiful if we humbly and patiently try to fit together all the information available to us from all possible sources.

Questions and Answers

Can science prove the existence of God?

No, science cannot prove the existence of God. This question is outside the realm of science.[16] First, science does not prove things true. It either proves them false or fails to prove them false. Second, science has a narrow window through which to view the universe. Scientific conclusions must be based on observation. Our five senses are the only receptors available to science. We can enhance them to some extent with instruments and tools, but we are still limited to a small spectrum of physical measurements and not to any spiritual measurements.

We can, however, find the existence of God in other ways. Plenty of evidence has been given to us for this very purpose.

"But ask now the beasts, and they shall teach thee; and the fowls of the air, and they shall tell thee:

"Or speak to the earth, and it shall teach thee: and the fishes of the sea shall declare unto thee.

"Who knoweth not in all these that the hand of the Lord hath wrought this?

"In whose hand is the soul of every living thing, and the breath of all mankind.

"Doth not the ear try words? and the mouth taste his meat?" (Job 12:7–10).

"And behold, all things have their likeness, and all things are created and made to bear record of me, both things which are temporal, and things which are spiritual; things which are in the heavens above, and things which are on the earth, and things which are in the earth, and things which are under the earth, both above and beneath: all things bear record of me" (Moses 6:63).

"Thou hast had signs enough; will ye tempt your God? Will ye say, Show unto me a sign, when ye have the testimony of all these thy brethren, and also all the holy prophets? The scriptures are laid before thee, yea, and all things denote there is a God; yea, even the earth, and all things that are upon the face of it, yea, and its motion, yea, and also all the planets which move in their regular form do witness that there is a Supreme Creator" (Alma 30:44).

Albert Einstein said, "What I see in nature is a magnificent structure that we can comprehend only very imperfectly, and that must fill a thinking person with a feeling of humility. This is a genuinely religious feeling...."

Revealed religion can prove the existence of God with certainty to anyone who wants to know. Christ's answer to Peter's testimony tells us that our Father in Heaven will give us this assurance.

"When Jesus came into the coasts of Caesarea Philippi, he asked his disciples, saying, Whom do men say that I the Son of man am?

"And they said, Some say that thou art John the Baptist: some, Elias; and others, Jeremias, or one of the prophets.

"He saith unto them, But whom say ye that I am?

"And Simon Peter answered and said, Thou art the Christ, the Son of the living God.

"And Jesus answered and said unto him, Blessed art thou, Simon Bar-jona: for flesh and blood hath not revealed it unto thee, but my Father which is in heaven" (Matthew 16:13–17).

As sure as this knowledge is to those who have it, many are not receptive to it.

> "But the natural man receiveth not the things of the Spirit of God: for they are foolishness unto him: neither can he know them, because they are spiritually discerned" (1 Corinthians 2:14).

Can science use Mormon doctrine?

It is difficult to transfer religious concepts directly to science; at the same time, it is important to try to do so. If scientists could understand all that has been given by revelation as a guide to their research, they would be starting much closer to the whole truth. From there, it would be easier to ferret out the details.

Scriptures and other religious teachings often contain layers of information that go much deeper than we can understand. As an example, the following summary of laws surely contains much that pertains to the way the universe works.

> "All kingdoms have a law given;
>
> "And there are many kingdoms; for there is no space in the which there is no kingdom; and there is no kingdom in which there is no space, either a greater or a lesser kingdom.
>
> "And unto every kingdom is given a law; and unto every law there are certain bounds also and conditions.
>
> "All beings who abide not in those conditions are not justified.
>
> "For intelligence cleaveth unto intelligence; wisdom receiveth wisdom; truth embraceth truth; virtue loveth virtue; light cleaveth unto light; mercy hath compassion on mercy and claimeth her own; justice continueth its course and claimeth its own; judgment goeth before the face of him who sitteth upon the throne and governeth and executeth all things.

"He comprehendeth all things, and all things are before him, and all things are round about him; and he is above all things, and in all things, and is through all things, and is round about all things; and all things are by him, and of him, even God, forever and ever.

"And again, verily I say unto you, he hath given a law unto all things, by which they move in their times and their seasons;

"And their courses are fixed, even the courses of the heavens and the earth, which comprehend the earth and all the planets.

"And they give light to each other in their times and in their seasons, in their minutes, in their hours, in their days, in their weeks, in their months, in their years—all these are one year with God, but not with man.

"The earth rolls upon her wings, and the sun giveth his light by day, and the moon giveth her light by night, and the stars also give their light, as they roll upon their wings in their glory, in the midst of the power of God" (D&C 88:36–47).

Though study of concepts such as priesthood power and spiritual dimensions associated with matter are beyond the abilities of science, this scripture and others contain much information that science can use. In this case, God presents laws that sound like science's physical laws to us.

This same section of the Doctrine and Covenants contains God's strong admonition to us to study everything. Much that is considered science is included among the doctrines of the kingdom discussed in these verses.

"And I give unto you a commandment that you shall teach one another the doctrine of the kingdom.

"Teach ye diligently and my grace shall attend you, that you may be instructed more perfectly in theory, in principle, in doctrine, in the law of the gospel, in all things that pertain unto the kingdom of God, that are expedient for you to understand;

"Of things both in heaven and in the earth, and under the earth; things which have been, things which are, things which must shortly come to pass; things which are at home, things which are abroad; the wars and the perplexities of the nations, and the judgments which are on the land; and a knowledge also of countries and of kingdoms" (D&C 88:77–79).

Will studying science destroy my testimony?

Richard Feynman was a prominent, Nobel Prize-winning physicist. Though not religious himself, he saw no conflict between science and religion. He gave an insightful and sympathetic analysis of the question presented here, that he recognized happens from time to time.

> "A young man of a religious family goes to the university, say, and studies science. As a consequence of his study of science, he begins, naturally to doubt, as it is necessary in his studies. So first he begins to doubt, and then he begins to disbelieve, perhaps, in his father's God. By 'God' I mean the kind of personal God, to which one prays, who has something to do with creation, as one prays for moral values, perhaps."[17]

A key element here is that it is his father's God that the young man doubts, not his own. Those who have strong personal testimonies, those whose parents' God has become their God, are protected. When they are presented with science or any other system of ideas, lack of a previously obtained and constantly growing testimony can be a problem.

Students need to know, as we all need to know, that science cannot disprove religion. Scientific questions should be dealt with by applying the scientific method. Science requires that we doubt all of science. This is the basis of continual progress in science. In science, we do experiments designed to prove things wrong.

Henry Eyring gave some advice about how parents and others can protect young people from loss of faith.

> "There is no harm in attempting to resolve apparently conflicting points of view, provided one is not taken in by one's own sophistry. There are few ways in which good people do more harm to those who take them seriously than to defend the gospel with arguments that won't hold water. Many of the difficulties encountered by young people going to college would be avoided if parents and teachers were more careful to distinguish between what they know to be true and what they think may be true. Impetuous youth, upon finding the authority it trusts crumbling, even on unimportant details, is apt to lump everything together and throw the baby out with the bath."[18]

Religion requires that we have faith. The kind of experiment prescribed by religion is very different from scientific experiments. Religious experiments are designed to build faith until that faith becomes knowledge, while scientific experiments are designed to test theories. The stronger our faith and testimony, the less likely we are to apply scientific doubt to religious questions.

Belief in religion and science is consistent. Francis Collins, director of the Human Genome Project that determined the order of the millions of bases in the human genome said:

> "In my view, there is no conflict in being a rigorous scientist and a person who believes in a God who takes a personal interest in each one of us. Science's domain is to explore nature. God's domain is in the spiritual world, a realm not possible to explore with the tools and language of science."[19]

Kenneth Miller, another prominent biological scientist said:

"True knowledge comes only from a combination of faith and reason. . . . What science cannot do is to assign either meaning or purpose to the world it explores. This leads some to conclude that the world as seen by science is devoid of meaning and absent of purpose. It is not. What it does mean is that our human tendencies to assign meaning and value must transcend science, and ultimately must come from outside of it. The science that results, I would suggest, is enriched and informed from its contact with the values and principles of faith. The God of Abraham does not tell us which proteins control the cell cycle. But He does give us reason to care, a reason to cherish that understanding, and above all a reason to prefer the light of knowledge to the darkness of ignorance."[20]

The last paragraph in Stephen Hawking's popular book *A Brief History of Time: From the Big Bang to Black Holes* recognizes God and expresses the idea that true success in science will occur when science and religion come together—when how will be combined with why.

"However, if we do discover a complete theory, it should in time be understandable by everyone, not just by a few scientists. Then we shall all, philosophers, scientists and just ordinary people, be able to take part in the discussion of the question of why it is that we and the universe exist. If we find the answer to that, it would be the ultimate triumph of human reason—for then we should know the mind of God."[21]

Can good Mormons be scientists and vice versa?

One of the first recognizable scientists in The Church of Jesus Christ of Latter-day Saints was Elder Orson Pratt. He was among those chosen as members of the first Quorum of the Twelve Apostles in this dispensation. He said of himself, "From 1836 to 1844 I occupied much of my leisure time in study, and made myself thoroughly acquainted with algebra, geometry, trigonometry, conic sections, differential and integral calculus, astronomy, and most of the physical sciences. These studies I pursued without the assistance of a teacher."[22]

In 1851–52, as an instructor at the University of Deseret (now University of Utah), he delivered a series of lectures on astronomy. By this time he was a recognized mathematician, having discovered, among other things, a law governing planetary rotation. In the 1880s a noted astronomer, Professor Proctor, stated that there were only four real mathematicians in the world and that Orson Pratt was one of them.[23]

From the time of Orson Pratt there have been many faithful Mormon scientists who have easily accommodated science and religious faith in their lives.[24] A few of these whose names are easily recognized by members of The Church of Jesus Christ of Latter-day Saints are James E. Talmage[25], John A. Widtsoe[26], and Henry Eyring[27].

Elder Richard G. Scott had a successful career as a nuclear engineer before being called to full-time church service. During the October 2007 general conference of The Church of Jesus Christ of Latter-day Saints, he compared the scientific and revealed-truth approaches to finding truth. He said:

> "There are two ways to find truth—both useful, provided we follow the laws upon which they are predicated. The first is the scientific method.... The scientific method is a valuable way of seeking truth. However, it has two limitations. First, we never can be sure we have identified absolute truth, though we often draw nearer and nearer to it. Second, sometimes, no matter how earnestly we apply the method, we can get the wrong answer.
>
> "The best way of finding truth is simply to go to the origin of all truth and ask or respond to inspiration. For success, two ingredients are essential: first, unwavering faith in the source of all truth; second, a willingness to

keep God's commandments to keep open spiritual communication with Him."[28]

The message of this book could not be stated better.

Why are we living on Earth?

Mormon doctrine is clear in proclaiming that each human being is a spirit son or daughter of God, housed in a physical body. Before birth, these spirits knew God as their Eternal Father and accepted His plan, by which each would obtain a physical body, gain earthly experience, and progress toward his or her eternal destiny.

> "Even before they were born, they, with many others, received their first lessons in the world of spirits and were prepared to come forth in the due time of the Lord" (D&C 138:56).

At death, these spirit children of God leave their physical bodies to await the resurrection, when spirit and body will be permanently united.

> "And we see that death comes upon mankind, yea, the death which has been spoken of by Amulek, which is the temporal death; nevertheless there was a space granted unto man in which he might repent; therefore this life became a probationary state; a time to prepare to meet God; a time to prepare for that endless state which has been spoken of by us, which is after the resurrection of the dead" (Alma 24:12).

Between obtaining a physical body and laying it down at death is a time for our other purposes on Earth. We are here to learn and to be tested. President Ezra Taft Benson summarized this phase of our existence:

> "When our Heavenly Father placed Adam and Eve on this earth, He did so with the purpose in mind of teaching them how to regain His presence. Our Father

promised a Savior to redeem them from their fallen condition. He gave to them the plan of salvation and told them to teach their children faith in Jesus Christ and repentance. Further, Adam and his posterity were commanded by God to be baptized, to receive the Holy Ghost, and to enter into the order of the Son of God . . . which is only received in the house of the Lord."[29]

The universe was made for a purpose. Jesus Christ, the firstborn of God the Father, created a place where the spirit children of His Father could have the important experiences of mortality. The earth on which we live, and the whole universe, are the result of matter and energy organized for our benefit.

> "And it came to pass that Moses called upon God, saying: Tell me, I pray thee, why these things are so, and by what thou madest them?
>
> "And behold, the glory of the Lord was upon Moses, so that Moses stood in the presence of God, and talked with him face to face. And the Lord God said unto Moses: For mine own purpose have I made these things. Here is wisdom and it remaineth in me.
>
> "And by the word of my power, have I created them, which is mine Only Begotten Son, who is full of grace and truth" (Moses 1:30–32).

We know little of what there is to know about the Earth or the universe of which it is a part. We know even less about the spiritual universe with which the physical universe is intimately associated. We do know that it is all part of an overarching effort made by God for us.

> "For behold, this is my work and my glory—to bring to pass the immortality and eternal life of man" (Moses 1:39).

What is our responsibility as stewards of the Earth?

The account of creation in Genesis contains a strong directive to humankind with regard to having dominion over and subduing the earth and everything on it.

> "And God said, Let us make man in our image, after our likeness: and let them have dominion over the fish of the sea, and over the fowl of the air, and over the cattle, and over all the earth, and over every creeping thing that creepeth upon the earth. . . .
>
> "And God blessed them, and God said unto them, Be fruitful, and multiply, and replenish the earth, and subdue it: and have dominion over the fish of the sea, and over the fowl of the air, and over every living thing that moveth upon the earth" (Genesis 1:26, 28).

It takes further explanation to get to the concept of stewardship.

> "Yea, all things which come of the earth, in the season thereof, are made for the benefit and the use of man, both to please the eye and to gladden the heart. . . .
>
> "And it pleaseth God that he hath given all these things unto man; for unto this end were they made to be used, with judgment, not to excess, neither by extortion" (D&C 59:18, 20).

> "For it is expedient that I, the Lord, should make every man accountable, as a steward over earthly blessings, which I have made and prepared for my creatures" (D&C 104:13).

Though there are still some problems, modern science has moved us far in the direction of producing food and other products while caring for the resources necessary for their production. By properly caring for the earth and using the tools provided by science, we are able to produce more each year. The areas of greatest environmental concern are where available scientific knowledge is not applied to production and resource management.

How much do we know about the universe?[30]

In the 1500s and 1600s, Copernicus[31], Kepler, and Newton unsettled cosmology by proposing that the earth is one of many planets orbiting one of many stars in a universe larger than had previously been imagined. In 1908, scientists thought our galaxy constituted the whole universe and that we were surrounded by a huge void. Edwin Hubble, for whom the Hubble telescope is named, had a revolutionary impact in the 1920s when he observed that the universe appears to be steadily expanding. At least to that point it was still possible to visualize a universe made of a combination of matter. We now know that our galaxy is one of more than four hundred billion galaxies in the universe.[32]

Now scientists are struggling with the observation that what can be detected as ordinary matter makes up less than five percent of the universe. Unless there is much more matter present than can be seen, there is not enough gravity in galaxies to keep the stars spinning around in them from flying away. The new term is dark matter. To add another level of complexity, that also requires dark matter to explain, objects in the universe are not evenly dispersed. Strings of galaxies weave through space.

When the characteristics of the universe mentioned above have been accounted for by adding unseen dark matter, only 30 percent of the universe is included. Recent observation that expansion of the universe is not steady, but is accelerating, requires even further explanation. The other 70 percent is proposed to be an antigravity force called dark energy.

Looking into the sky may be the most inspiring manifestation of God's creations. The added scientific insights now beginning to come into focus only add to the picture. Correlation in our minds between revelations that mention planets, stars, and so forth and scientific observations and theories clarifies both views. Who could not be awestruck by Moses's great vision of the heavens and the earth?

> "And it came to pass that Moses called upon God, saying: Tell me, I pray thee, why these things are so, and by what thou madest them?
>
> "And behold, the glory of the Lord was upon Moses, so that Moses stood in the presence of God, and talked with him face to face. And the Lord God said unto Moses: For mine own purpose have I made these things. Here is wisdom and it remaineth in me.
>
> "And by the word of my power, have I created them, which is mine Only Begotten Son, who is full of grace and truth.
>
> "And worlds without number have I created; and I also created them for mine own purpose; and by the Son I created them, which is mine Only Begotten.
>
> "And the first man of all men have I called Adam, which is many.
>
> "But only an account of this earth, and the inhabitants thereof, give I unto you. For behold, there are many worlds that have passed away by the word of my power. And there are many that now stand, and innumerable are they unto man; but all things are numbered unto me, for they are mine and I know them" (Moses 1:30:35).

Possibly most inspiring of all is the realization that among all His creations, God cares about each of us individually. Enoch realized this and said:

> "And were it possible that man could number the particles of the earth, yea, millions of earths like this, it would not be a beginning to the number of thy creations; and thy curtains are stretched out still; and yet thou art there, and thy bosom is there; and also thou art just; thou art merciful and kind forever" (Moses 7:30).

Can science show that life began by chance?

Many of the most interesting theories, including some important hypotheses concerning life and its origin, do not lend themselves to examination by science. The idea that life began spontaneously is a good example. Usually the question is, "Did life begin spontaneously and undirected from a mixture of chemicals and energy?"

What is required to test such a theory? An experiment must be designed with the aim of disproving the theory, not proving it. Since the conditions and mixture of chemicals present are unknown at the time the theory suggests the initial reactions leading to life occurred, a best guess from all available evidence is as close as we can come. An example showing that a mixture of chemicals reacts to produce "life-related" molecules will not do. Innumerable combinations of chemicals and conditions can do that. Even more combinations of chemicals and conditions fail to produce such molecules or to react at all.

A more serious problem is the requirement for undirected spontaneity. Our experiment must be designed with no intelligent intervention, even our own. This cannot be done. We decide the mixture of chemicals and the conditions.

Since the theory cannot be tested for these and possibly other reasons, it stands as a theory. Efforts to prove the theory demonstrate the commitment to the theory of those who do so, but such efforts do not convert the theory into a fact.

Who was Adam?

The various philosophies and religions in the world now and in the past have given overlapping but slightly different answers to this question. The Latter-day Saint answer says that Adam was the first of the human race and that Adam and his wife, Eve, were the ancestral parents of all people on earth.

"And the first man of all men have I called Adam, which is many" (Moses 1:34).

"And Adam called his wife's name Eve, because she was the mother of all living; for thus have I, the Lord God, called the first of all women, which are many" (Moses 4:26).

There is no room for wavering on this subject. Beyond his being the first human, Adam has additional credentials. He is known in the scriptures by titles other than Adam.

"And also with Michael, or Adam, the father of all, the prince of all, the ancient of days" (D&C 27:11).

As Michael, Adam joined with Jesus Christ in creating the earth.

"Adam . . . is Michael the Archangel, spoken of in the Scriptures. Then to Noah, who is Gabriel; he stands next in authority to Adam in the Priesthood; he was called of God to this office, and was the father of all living in his day, and to him was given the dominion. These men held keys first on earth, and then in heaven.

"The Priesthood is an everlasting principle, and existed with God from eternity, and will to eternity, without beginning of days or end of years. The keys have to be brought from heaven whenever the Gospel is sent. When they are revealed from heaven, it is by Adam's authority.

"Daniel in his seventh chapter speaks of the Ancient of Days; he means the oldest man, our Father Adam, Michael; he will call his children together and hold a council with them to prepare them for the coming of the Son of Man. He (Adam) is the father of the human family, and presides over the spirits of all men, and all that have had the keys must stand before him in this grand council. This may take place before some of us leave this stage of action. The Son of Man stands before him, and there is given him glory and dominion. Adam delivers up his stewardship to Christ, that which was delivered to him as holding the keys of the universe, but retains his standing as head of the human family."[33]

What is the Church's stand on the origin of man?

This question carries an assumption that there should be an official policy on every topic, which is not the case. There is not a black or white, "approved" policy on every topic.

Since this question is asked so frequently, the First Presidency has published clarifications from time to time to guide Church members in their thinking. A compilation of these statements that is made available to students at Brigham Young University is reprinted in Appendix II. It contains only statements from the First Presidency. And article from the *Encyclopedia of Mormonism* is included because the "First Presidency Minutes" item included in it is not otherwise available to the public. The final packet was approved in 1992 by BYU's Board of Trustees, consisting of the First Presidency, members of the Quorum of the Twelve, and other general authorities and officers of The Church of Jesus Christ of Latter-day Saints.

From the *Encyclopedia of Mormonism* article, we read that we are children of God:

> "The Church of Jesus Christ of Latter-day Saints, basing its belief on divine revelation, ancient and modern, declares man to be the direct and lineal offspring of Deity.... Man is the child of God, formed in the divine image and endowed with divine attributes."[34]

We are then told that we should be able to agree with the then First Presidency of Joseph F. Smith, John R. Winder, and Anthon H. Lund that "Adam is the primal parent of our race."[35] We learn in the scriptures something about why we were created but not how.

"And worlds without number have I created; and I also created them for mine own purpose; and by my Son I created them, which is mine Only Begotten.

"But only an account of this earth, and the inhabitants thereof, give I unto you. For behold, there are many worlds that have passed away by the word of my power. And there are many that now stand, and innumerable are they unto man; but all things are numbered unto me, for they are mine and I know them" (Moses 1:33, 35).

We are promised that when the Lord comes again He will tell us how we were created:

"Yea, verily I say unto you, in that day when the Lord shall come, he shall reveal all things—

"Things which have passed, and hidden things which no man knew, things of the earth, by which it was made, and the purpose and the end thereof—

"Things most precious, things that are above, and things that are beneath, things that are in the earth, and upon the earth, and in heaven" (D&C 101:32–34).

What is evolution?

Many observations for many years led to the theory of evolution. Evidence that the earth is very old is everywhere. Things that do not live now once lived on our planet. Children look like their parents. Agriculture wages a constant battle to stay ahead of newly emerging varieties of weeds, diseases, and other pests. Farmers take advantage of the processes they see in nature to carefully breed crops and animals with constantly improve traits. Each year's flu vaccine has to be different than the previous year's vaccine because the virus is different each year. This list could go on for pages. How can these things be explained?

Science's theory to explain many of these things is evolution. The theory has changed slowly over time as it has been tested and new information has emerged. It continues to be tested and to change. No one thinks the final version has been reached.

In biology, evolution is the explanation of the process by which populations of organisms acquire and pass on novel traits from generation to generation.[36] The development of the theory of evolution began with the introduction of the concept of natural selection in an 1858 paper by Charles Darwin and Alfred Russel Wallace and in Darwin's 1859 book, *The Origin of Species*. Darwin and Wallace proposed that evolution occurs because heritable traits that increase an individual's chance of successfully reproducing will become more common, by inheritance, from one generation to the next; likewise, heritable traits that decrease an individual's chance of reproducing will become more rare. The theory also postulates that all species evolved from less-complicated organisms, and that individual species change over time. Because of its potential implications for the origins of humankind, the theory has been at the center of many social and religious controversies since its inception.[37]

It is not surprising that Joseph Smith taught about reproduction and heredity fifteen years before Charles Darwin published the first of his thoughts on these concepts:

"God has set many signs on the earth, as well as in the heavens; for instance, the oak of the forest, the fruit of the tree, the herb of the field—all bear a sign that seed hath been planted there; for it is a decree of the Lord that every tree, plant, and herb bearing seed should bring forth of its kind, and cannot come forth after any other law or principle."[38]

Should we study evolution?

We should study every scientific theory, including evolution, and many other subjects.

"Teach ye diligently and my grace shall attend you, that you may be instructed more perfectly in theory, in principle, in doctrine, in the law of the gospel, in all things that pertain unto the kingdom of God, that are expedient for you to understand;

"Of things both in heaven and in the earth, and under the earth; things which have been, things which are, things which must shortly come to pass; things which are at home, things which are abroad; the wars and the perplexities of the nations, and the judgments which are on the land; and a knowledge also of countries and of kingdoms" (D&C 88:78–79).

A prominent scientist at Brigham Young University addressed this topic as follows:

"To me, evolution is simply the scientific study of the underlying mechanics of the creative process. It studies the patterns of creation and seeks to define the processes which gave rise to these patterns. It does not preclude the existence of God, nor does it challenge His role in the creation. I ask, 'What does the creative process teach me about the nature of the Creator?' My studies lead me to believe that not only did the Lord create the earth, but that He did so in a supremely intelligent fashion.

"I believe the Lord set certain laws which resulted in a world filled with diversity, beauty, and form; each species interacting with every other, tied together in a glorious whole. I do not understand what all these laws are, which is why I study the things I do.

"So what do we do when some ideas in evolutionary theory seem to contradict the doctrines of the Church, or when people around us seem unsettled by ideas they find hard to reconcile?

"Let me suggest that we should be humble.

"Let's not insist that we must have all of the answers and have them now. Let's not demand that the Lord reveal it now or that the scientists stop studying it now. Let's stop thinking that we know more than we do. The Lord has not yet revealed the mechanics of creation. And scientists are still probing around in the dark, the best we can, to try and understand even the basics of the creative process. In the meantime, let's be humble and grateful to live in a world which inspires such deep contemplation."[39]

Many public arguments about evolution (and many other topics) occur between people who understand much more about their own point of view than about their opponent's point of view. Some effort on both sides to learn about each other's point of view would add considerably to understanding. Henry Eyring commented on this mutual ignorance problem as follows:

> "There are lots of things, of course, that science does not know, but to me the saddest thing I see is people who feel that science threatens them religiously. It could not possibly threaten us religiously, because the same God who 'made' our religion, that same God is making the universe. Science might threaten our understanding of religion. I am not doubting that—that some of us, including me, have such faulty understanding of our religion that almost anything might threaten it. But the thing that is important about that is if we want to influence our sons and daughters, we must get our religion in the kind of shape that it cannot be threatened by anything that science discovers or does not discover."[40]

What is creationism?

"Creationism is the idea that God created all living and nonliving things in more or less present form and that humans and apes do not share a common ancestor."[41] Because it is not testable by scientific methods, creationism is classified not as science, but as religion.

Most who hold creationism beliefs consider such beliefs to be a part of religious faith. They often reject popular views of science and certain scientific theories in particular. Most notable is the rejection of evolution and its implications for current evolutionary biology.[42]

The term creationism carries more meaning than is seen in its definition. It is used in public and political battles over having the creation story from the scriptures taught in school science classes in place of (or at least along with) evolution.[43] Many smaller disagreements are imbedded within this struggle. People argue about interpretation of the scriptures—things such as twenty-four-hour days versus periods of time. Though it is not part of the Creation, Noah's flood is often another point of contention.

These struggles will probably continue for a long time. The dangers of teaching religion as science might be greater than the advantages some see in doing so. Proponents of teaching creationism in public schools are not satisfied with suggestions that creationism be taught in nonscience parts of the curriculum. Questions about the wisdom of teaching religion in public schools rarely arises in creationism battles.

Science and religion need not be viewed as threats to each other. They can be complementary ways of approaching the truth we all seek. Better efforts could be made to help students understand the scientific method and the resulting fragile nature of scientific "discoveries." Science is sometimes criticized for its ever-changing conclusions. Such inability to make up its mind is the essence of scientific inquiry.

What is intelligent design?

Intelligent design is a recent term used to reformulate creationism in a more science-sounding way.

> "Intelligent design is the idea that the complexity of living things, and the low probability of evolution producing such complexity, can only be explained by the existence and involvement of an intelligent designer."[44]

Though intelligent design sounds like simple recognition of direction from a higher intelligence, it is much more. It is a charged political term that is taking the place of creationism (or, more recently, creation science) in political arguments. Though it might seem so, recognizing God's role in creation is not equivalent to agreeing with the intelligent design concept.

The intelligent design movement, which began in the early 1990s, is promoted by a conservative Christian think tank called the Discovery Institute. It is an organized campaign with a goal of restating creationism in nonreligious terms and without appeals to scripture. It is thought that such an approach will be better received by policy makers, educators, the public, and even by the scientific community.[45]

Intelligent design asks science to do something it cannot do.[46] The questions it poses are not within the realm of scientific investigation. The huge number of scientists who recognize God as the Creator came to that conclusion in the realm of religion. Though their observations of the wonders of the universe support their religious beliefs, their faith is not a result of the scientific method of seeking truth. If it were, their faith would be no more than a theory open to constant efforts to disprove it.

Will we always have enough food?[47]

In 1798, Thomas Malthus published "An Essay on the Principle of Population," surmising that population growth would always outrun food production. At that time, about five acres of land was required to produce enough food for each of the earth's approximately one billion people. Today, more than six billion people eat from about half an acre each.48 How did this tenfold increase in production happen?

Among the many steps taken to keep food available were a few giant steps. One of these was the introduction of hybrid vigor in plant breeding. Another was discovery of a process for capturing nitrogen from air to make ammonia, including that used in nitrogen fertilizer. The biggest single leap forward was the Green Revolution of the 1940s, 1950s and 1960s. Genes bred into cereal crops by laboriously crossbreeding thousands of plant varieties from around the world made it possible to save more than one billion people from starvation.

Another revolution has begun that will dwarf those that preceded it. With the ability to map and understand genes, now we can give specific desired characteristics to plants, animals, and microorganisms. Instead of long, hit-and-miss, trial-and-error processes, we can select specific genes and insert them where they are needed. We can even use more than one copy of a gene, and we can turn genes on and off to suit our needs. These powerful tools make it possible to protect against diseases, insects, and drought and to improve the nutritional content of food.[49]

Unlike the Green Revolution, the Gene Revolution goes far beyond food and agriculture. We now have a complete map of the human genome. This is more information than we have ever had about our own genetic makeup. A string of research results based on this information is now moving toward everyday application, including information describing how to cure and how to prevent diseases previously out of our reach.

Recently, Norman Borlaug, the father of the Green Revolution, commented in the *Wall Street Journal* on the Gene Revolution.[50] Among other things he said:

> "Since 1996, the planting of genetically modified crops developed through biotechnology has spread to about 250 million acres . . . around the world. . . .
>
> "In each of the last six years, biotech cotton saved U.S. farmers from using 93 million gallons of water in water-scarce areas, 2.4 million gallons of fuel and 41,000 person-days to apply the pesticides. . . .
>
> "Agricultural science and technology, including the indispensable tools of biotechnology, will be critical to meeting the growing demands for food, feed, fiber and biofuels. . . . This flourishing new branch of science extends to food crops, fuels, fibers, livestock and even forest products."

This is just the beginning. The Gene Revolution still has a long way to go, but it is off to a great start. In 2008, U.S. farmers used genetically modified seeds for 73 percent of the corn, 87 percent of the cotton, and 91 percent of the soybeans planted.[51] Milk is coagulated to make cheese by an enzyme originally extracted from the stomachs of young calves but now raised in yeast cells containing calf genes. The rest of the world is beginning to share in the benefits of this new revolution.

Malthus was not the last to conclude that the earth was incapable of producing enough to feed everyone. It has been common at least since his time for people to suggest that the way to feed and provide for everyone is to make sure there are fewer people. This *solution* is still being suggested.[52] It seems to be difficult for many to accept God's explanation of the situation:

> "For the earth is full, and there is enough and to spare; yea, I prepared all things, and have given unto the children of men to be agents unto themselves" (D&C 104:17).

Science and technology have allowed us to keep up with population growth and to improve diets beyond anything imaginable two hundred years ago. If the technology available today were applied everywhere, everyone on earth would be well fed. However, even today's technology will not be enough by 2050, when there will be approximately nine billion people to feed. It is incumbent upon us to make sure that available technology is employed to feed those living now and to continue the work that will provide the necessary science and technology to feed those who come after us.[53]

Are the brain and the mind the same thing?

The human brain may be the most complex of all organs found in nature. Rapid progress is being made in the field of neuroscience, which is the understanding of the brain and its functions.[54] Though there is still a long way to go, useful results of studies are becoming available.

Knowing whether the brain and the mind are the same thing is harder than knowing how the brain works. Latter-day Saints (and many other people) believe in life after death. So the question could be rephrased to ask if our memories go with us after this life? Our religion tells us that we will know those we knew in this life and remember what we did here. This concept is not testable by science, but it does make us look differently at science's discoveries about the brain, memory, consciousness, and so forth.

Will scientists ever be able to create life?

To answer this question we have to start with a more basic question. What is life? It is easy to agree that people live. Animals clearly live too. However, the richness of life for people exceeds that of animals by a huge margin. We say that plants live too, but their lives are different than the lives of animals. We could break these categories down even further, such as into all the various forms of animal and plant life. We could also talk about insects. But let's move on to microorganisms.

Most people are familiar with things like bacteria or yeast. These have their own genetic material and their own tools for both growing and making more of themselves. Surely this is life, even though it is far from human life. As we go on in our search of life, we soon come to viruses. Deciding whether viruses live or not is difficult. They have their own genetic material but not the machinery to process it to make or to replicate themselves. They must invade some of the living things mentioned above to find machinery to read their genetic codes. They then replicate in huge numbers, even without being able to do so by themselves.

We could next look at plasmids. These are tiny pieces of genetic material found in organisms such as bacteria. They multiply and get passed on to new generations of their host organisms. Are they living, or are they more like viruses, or are they part of the organisms in which they live?

To go one more step, we should mention prions. These are just tiny pieces of protein material. They do not even have genetic material of their own. It would be hard to say that they live. However, they cause things like mad cow disease.

Now we can talk about whether scientists will ever be able to create life. Some things we hear about, such as cloning, make it sound as if life has been created. Cloning is an example of gathering all the necessary pieces from living things and borrowing all the machinery to carry out the work. It is similar to embryo-transplant procedures with a few added twists. It is even possible to create exact physical duplicates in this way, but this is not creation of life from scratch. At this level most scientists begin to wonder about ethics. For example, there is a huge difference between using cloning to make Dolly the sheep and doing the same thing with humans.

The polio virus has been created synthetically in a laboratory. There is still the question of whether viruses are living things. Recently scientists have made from scratch the genetic material for a bacterium called *Mycoplasma genitalium,* the smallest bacterium that can be grown in the laboratory.[55] Outside of the laboratory this bacterium causes urinary tract infections. There is still a long way to go before this genome is shown to be active and is made to replicate itself. This will be done by replacing the genetic material in another cell with the newly sequenced material. At this stage of research, this is an expensive and difficult way to do something that happens on its own. Once it has been done, the objective is to make cells that can produce biofuels or pharmaceuticals, invade cancer calls and destroy them, clean up oil spills, and an endless list of other things. However, what is being created is a way to tailor-make cells by manipulation of known genes. This will be much more efficient than selecting cells for specific traits in the traditional way. What is not being done is creation of life from scratch.

Appendix I— Some Abandoned Scientific Theories

The core of the scientific method is the idea that theories about how things are can be proven false or not proven false, but can never be proven true. If an experiment disproves a theory, a new theory is developed to explain what has been observed. This method slowly eliminates theories and replaces them with better theories. The longer this process continues, the closer the new theories are to the truth. The following is a good summary of this process.

"Some hypotheses—indeed some full-fledged theories—are simply defunct science: in their day they represented the cutting-edge of theoretical science but they've since been superseded by other versions that accord more accurately with reality, or they've been realized to be totally at odds with reality and been replaced wholesale by something that is at least, so far as we can establish, closer to the truth. As science slowly evolves—as our knowledge of the universe slowly progresses in the direction of completeness, even if as yet maybe nowhere approaching that ideal closely—ideas and hypotheses from seemingly different disciplines suddenly take on new relationships: can be seen as the myriad pieces of a single, very large jigsaw. Those pieces that simply will not fit, no matter how much we manipulate them, naturally come under greatest scrutiny."[56]

Below are a few examples of the many scientific theories that served as the best available explanation of what was observed until a better theory was found. From our vantage point today, some of these may look ridiculous. However, if we had lived at an earlier time, they would have seemed as reasonable to us as do our present ideas. Thinking of what the explanations we accept today will look like in the future should humble to us.

Astronomical Theories

The Ptolemaic system, favored by Aristotle and Ptolemy, had the earth at the center of the universe with everything else rotating around it. Copernicus replaced this theory with the heliocentric system, with the planets rotating around the sun[57]. Newton's universal gravitation, with everything attracting everything else, changed the celestial logic again. Finally, for now, Einstein's ideas about general relativity changed it all again.[58]

Aristotle's Physics

Aristotle had a theory of gravity to explain why some things fall downward and other things, like steam, fall upward. He also taught that the elements that make up the earth (earth, air, water, and fire) are different from those that make up the heavens. A system of relationships among these elements explained much that is observed. This theory lasted for more than two thousand years but was gradually supplanted by more robust theories proposed by Galileo, Descartes, Newton, and others.

Alchemy

Aristotle's earth, air, water, and fire ideas were the foundation of the long-accepted concepts of alchemy. Aristotle taught that there is only one kind of matter but that it can take many forms. The four fundamental forms are earth, air, water, and fire. Since all elements are of the same kind of matter but just in different forms, they should be able to be transformed into each other. Hence, great efforts were made for many years to perform transformations such as lead into gold.

Atomic Theory

The concept that matter is composed of discrete units and cannot be divided into smaller units is thousands of years old. Democritus (460–370 B.C.) pictured such particles as the constituents of matter. They were named atoms, from the Greek word for indivisible.[59] These ideas were founded on philosophical reasoning rather than on experimentation and empirical observation.

Starting with the discovery of electrons by the English physicist J. J. Thompson (1856–1940), atoms began to be viewed as other than homogeneous particles. The idea of a sun-and-planet-type model gradually gave way to other models until a model with clouds of electrons surrounding a nucleus of protons and neutrons was proposed. This has been modified further to account for subunits of the subunits within atoms.[60]

Each of these changes was caused by the inability of a theory to withstand experimental challenges.[61] Through all these versions of the atom, scientists explained observations in physics and chemistry based on the theory current at their time.

Spontaneous Generation

Spontaneous generation says that living things appear spontaneously. This explained everything from mice appearing in a pile of dirty rags thrown in a corner to maggots on meat. It was believed by almost everyone, including Aristotle, for hundreds of years. Then, in the nineteenth century, Louis Pasteur designed and ran an experiment that easily proved it wrong. The current theory, which has held its own since Pasteur, is referred to as "all life from the living." Mice come from other mice, bacteria from other bacteria, and so forth.[62]

Miasma Theory of Disease

This theory started in the Middle Ages. It blamed diseases on miasma, a kind of smelly mist or vapor in the air that contained decomposed matter. During the mid-1800s, cholera outbreaks in London and Paris were blamed on miasmas. Among others, Florence Nightingale was a proponent of this theory. The miasma theory was consistent with the observations that disease was associated with poor sanitation and that sanitary improvements reduced disease. It is not consistent, however, with the observations of microbiology that led to the current germ theory of disease.[63]

Appendix II— Origin of Man Packet

Evolution and the Origin of Man

This packet contains, as far as could be found, all statements issued by the First Presidency of The Church of Jesus Christ of Latter-day Saints on the subject of evolution and the origin of man, and a statement on the Church's attitude toward science. The earliest First Presidency statement, "The Origin of Man," was issued during the administration of President Joseph F. Smith in 1909. This was followed by a First Presidency message in 1910 that included brief comments related to the study of these topics. The second statement, "Mormon View of Evolution," was issued during the administration of President Heber J. Grant in 1925. There has never been a formal declaration from the First Presidency addressing the general matter of organic evolution as a process for development of biological species, but these documents make clear the official position of the Church regarding the origin of man.

This packet also contains the article on evolution from the *Encyclopedia of Mormonism,* published in 1992. The current First Presidency authorized inclusion of the excerpt from the First Presidency minutes of 1931 in the 1992 *Encyclopedia* article.

Various views have been expressed by other Church leaders on this subject over many decades; however, formal statements by the First Presidency are the definitive source of official

Church positions. It is hoped that these materials will provide a firm foundation for individual study in a context of faith in the restored gospel.

Approved by the BYU Board of Trustees, June 1992.
IMPROVEMENT ERA
Vol. XIII, November 1909, No. 1

Editor's Table
"The Origin of Man"

BY THE FIRST PRESIDENCY OF THE CHURCH.

"God created man in his own image."

Inquiries arise from time to time respecting the attitude of The Church of Jesus Christ of Latter-day Saints upon questions which, though not vital from a doctrinal standpoint, are closely connected with the fundamental principles of salvation. The latest inquiry of this kind that has reached us is in relation to the origin of man. It is believed that a statement of the position held by the Church upon this important subject will be timely and productive of good.

In presenting the statement that follows we are not conscious of putting forth anything essentially new; neither is it our desire so to do. Truth is what we wish to present, and truth—eternal truth—is fundamentally old. A restatement of the original attitude of the Church relative to this matter is all that will be attempted here. To tell the truth as God has revealed it, and commend it to the acceptance of those who need to conform their opinions thereto, is the sole purpose of this presentation.

"God created man in his own image, in the image of God created he him; male and female created he them." In these plain and pointed words the inspired author of the book of Genesis made known to the world the truth concerning the origin of the human family. Moses, the prophet historian, "learned," as we are told, "in all the wisdom of the Egyptians," when making this important announcement, was not voicing a mere opinion, a theory derived from his researches into the occult lore of that ancient people. He was speaking as the mouthpiece of God, and his solemn declaration was for all time and for all people. No subsequent revelator of the truth has contradicted the great leader and lawgiver of Israel. All who have since spoken by divine authority upon this theme have confirmed his simple and sublime proclamation. Nor could it be otherwise. Truth has but one source, and all revelations from heaven are harmonious with each other. The omnipotent Creator, the maker of heaven and earth, had shown unto Moses everything pertaining to this planet, including the facts relating to man's origin, and the authoritative pronouncement of that mighty prophet and seer to the house of Israel, and through Israel to the whole world, is couched in the simple clause: "God created man in his own image" (Genesis 1:27; Moses 1:27–41).

The creation was two-fold—firstly, spiritual; secondly, temporal. This truth, also, Moses plainly taught—much more plainly than it has come down to us in the imperfect translations of the Bible that are now in use. Therein the fact of a spiritual creation, antedating the temporal creation, is strongly implied, but the proof of it is not so clear and conclusive as in other records held by the Latter-day Saints to be of equal authority with the Jewish scriptures. The partial obscurity of the latter upon the point in question is owing, no doubt, to the loss of those "plain and precious" parts of sacred writ, which, as the Book of Mormon informs us, have been taken away from the

Bible during its passage down the centuries (1 Nephi 13:24–29). Some of these missing parts the Prophet Joseph Smith undertook to restore when he revised those scriptures by the spirit of revelation, the result being that more complete account of the creation which is found in the book of Moses, previously cited. Note the following passages:

> "And now, behold I say unto you, that these are the generations of the heaven and the earth, when they were created in the day that I, the Lord God, made the heaven and the earth,
>
> "And every plant of the field before it was in the earth, and every herb of the field before it grew. For I, the Lord God, created all things, of which I have spoken, spiritually, before they were naturally upon the face of the earth. For I, the Lord God, had not caused it to rain upon the face of the earth. And I, the Lord God, had created all the children of men, and not yet a man to till the ground; for in heaven created I them, and there was not yet flesh upon the earth, neither in the water, neither in the air.
>
> "But I, the Lord God, spake, and there went up a mist from the earth, and watered the whole face of the ground.
>
> "And I, the Lord God, formed man from the dust of the ground, and breathed into his nostrils the breath of life; and man became a living soul, the first flesh upon the earth, the first man also; nevertheless, all things were before created, but spiritually were they created and made, according to my word" (Moses 3:4–7; see also chapters 1 and 2, and compare with Gen. 1 and 2).

These two points being established, namely, the creation of man in the image of God and the twofold character of the creation, let us now inquire: What was the form of man, in the spirit and in the body, as originally created? In a general way the answer is given in the words chosen as the text of this treatise. "God created man in his own image. It is more explicitly rendered in the Book of Mormon thus: "All men were created in the beginning after mine own image" (Ether 3: 15). It is the Father who is speaking. If, therefore, we can ascertain the form of the "Father of spirits," "The God of the spirits of all flesh," we shall be able to discover the form of the original man.

Jesus Christ, the Son of God, is "the express image" of His Father's person (Hebrews 1:3). He walked the earth as a human being, as a perfect man, and said, in answer to a question put to Him: "He that hath seen me hath seen the Father" (John 14:9). This alone ought to solve the problem to the satisfaction of every thoughtful, reverent mind. The conclusion is irresistible, that if the Son of God be the express image (that is, likeness) of His Father's person, then His Father is in the form of man; for that was the form of the Son of God, not only during His mortal life, but before His mortal birth, and after His resurrection. It was in this form that the Father and the Son, as two personages, appeared to Joseph Smith, when, as a boy of fourteen years, he received his first vision. Then if God made man—the first man—in His own image and likeness, he must have made him like unto Christ, and consequently like unto men of Christ's time and of the present day. That man was made in the image of Christ is positively stated in the Book of Moses:

> "And I, God, said unto mine Only Begotten, which was with me from the beginning, Let us make man in our image, after our likeness; and it was so. . . .
> "And I, God, created man in mine own image, in the image of mine Only Begotten created I him, male and female created I them" (Moses 2:26, 27).

The Father of Jesus is our Father also. Jesus Himself taught this truth, when He instructed His disciples how to pray: "Our Father which art in heaven," etc. Jesus, however, is the firstborn among all the sons of God—the first begotten in the spirit, and the only begotten in the flesh. He is our elder brother, and we, like Him, are in the image of God. All men and women are in the similitude of the universal Father and Mother, and are literally the sons and daughters of Deity.

"God created man in His own image." This is just as true of the spirit as it is of the body, which is only the clothing of the spirit, its complement; the two together constituting the soul. The spirit of man is in the form of man, and the spirits of all creatures are in the likeness of their bodies. This was plainly taught by the Prophet Joseph Smith (D&C 77:2).

Here is further evidence of the fact. More than seven hundred years before Moses was shown the things pertaining to this earth, another great prophet, known to us as the brother of Jared, was similarly favored by the Lord. He was even permitted to behold the spirit-body of the foreordained Savior, prior to His incarnation; and so like the body of a man was His spirit in form and appearance, that the prophet thought he was gazing upon a being of flesh and blood. He first saw the finger and then the entire body of the Lord—all in the spirit. The Book of Mormon says of this wonderful manifestation:

> "And it came to pass that when the brother of Jared had said these words, behold, the Lord stretched forth His hand and touched the stones one by one with His finger. And the veil was taken from off the eyes of the brother of Jared, and he saw the finger of the Lord; and it was as the finger of a man, like unto flesh and blood; and the brother of Jared fell down before the Lord, for he was struck with fear.
>
> "And the Lord saw that the brother of Jared had fallen to the earth; and the Lord said unto him, Arise, why hast thou fallen?
>
> "And he saith unto the Lord: I saw the finger of the Lord, and I feared lest he should smite me; for I knew not that the Lord had flesh and blood.

"And the Lord said unto him: Because of thy faith thou hast seen that I shall take upon me flesh and blood; and never has man come before me with such exceeding faith as thou hast; for were it not so ye could not have seen my finger. Sawest thou more than this?

"And he answered: Nay; Lord, show thyself unto me.

"And the Lord said unto him: Believest thou the works which I shall speak?

"And he answered: Yea, Lord, I know that thou speakest the truth, for thou art a God of truth, and canst not lie.

"And when he had said these words, behold, the Lord showed himself unto him, and said: Because thou knowest these things ye are redeemed from the fall; therefore ye are brought back into my presence; therefore I show myself unto you.

"Behold, I am He who was prepared from the foundation of the world to redeem my people. Behold, I am Jesus Christ. I am the Father and the Son. In me shall all mankind have light, and that eternally, even they who shall believe on my name; and they shall become my sons and my daughters.

"And never have I showed myself unto man whom I have created, for never hath man believed in me as thou hast. Seest thou that ye are created after mine own image? Yea, even all men were created in the beginning after mine own image.

"Behold, this body, which ye now behold, is the body of my spirit; and man have I created after the body of my spirit; and even as I appear unto thee to be in the spirit will I appear unto my people in the flesh" (Ether 3:6–16).

What more is needed to convince us that man, both in spirit and in body, is the image and likeness of God, and that God Himself is in the form of man?

When the divine Being whose spirit-body the brother of Jared beheld, took upon Him flesh and blood, He appeared as a man, having "body, parts and passions," like other men, though vastly superior to all others, because He was God, even the Son of God, the Word made flesh: in Him "dwelt the fulness of the Godhead bodily." And why should He not appear as a man? That was the form of His spirit, and it must needs have an appropriate covering, a suitable tabernacle. He came into the world as He had promised to come (3 Nephi 1:13), taking an infant tabernacle, and developing it gradually to the fulness of His spirit stature. He came as man had been coming for ages, and as man has continued to come ever since. Jesus, however, as shown, was the only begotten of God in the flesh.

Adam, our great progenitor, "the first man," was, like Christ, a premortal spirit, and like Christ he took upon him an appropriate body, the body of a man, and so became a "living soul." The doctrine of premortality—revealed so plainly, particularly in latter days—pours a wonderful flood of light upon the otherwise mysterious problem of man's origin. It shows that man, as a spirit, was begotten and born of heavenly parents, and reared to maturity in the eternal mansions of the Father, prior to coming upon the earth in a temporal body to undergo an experience in mortality. It teaches that all men existed in the spirit before any man existed in the flesh, and that all who have inhabited the earth since Adam have taken bodies and become souls in like manner.

It is held by some that Adam was not the first man upon this earth, and that the original human being was a development from lower orders of the animal creation. These, however, are the theories of men. The word of the Lord declares that Adam was "the first man of all men" (Moses 1:34), and we are therefore in duty bound to regard him as the primal parent of our race. It was shown to the brother of Jared that all men were created in the beginning after the image of God; and whether we take this to mean the spirit or the body, or both, it commits us to the same conclusion: Man began life as a human being, in the likeness of our heavenly Father.

True it is that the body of man enters upon its career as a tiny germ or embryo, which becomes an infant, quickened at a certain stage by the spirit whose tabernacle it is, and the child, after being born, develops into a man. There is nothing in this, however, to indicate that the original man, the first of our race, began life as anything less than a man, or less than the human germ or embryo that becomes a man.

Man, by searching, cannot find out God. Never, unaided, will he discover the truth about the beginning of human life. The Lord must reveal Himself, or remain unrevealed; and the same is true of the facts relating to the origin of Adam's race—God alone can reveal them. Some of these facts, however, are already known, and what has been made known it is our duty to receive and retain.

The Church of Jesus Christ of Latter-day Saints, basing its belief on divine revelation, ancient and modern, proclaims man to be the direct and lineal offspring of Deity. God Himself is an exalted man, perfected, enthroned, and supreme. By His almighty power He organized the earth, and all that it contains, from spirit and element, which exist co-eternally with Himself. He formed every plant that grows, and every animal that breathes, each after its own kind, spiritually and temporally—"that which is spiritual being in the likeness of that which is temporal, and that which is temporal in the likeness of that which is spiritual." He made the tadpole and the ape, the lion and the elephant; but He did not make them in His own image, nor endow them with Godlike reason and intelligence. Nevertheless, the whole animal creation will be perfected and perpetuated in the Hereafter, each class in its "distinct order or sphere," and will enjoy "eternal felicity." That fact has been made plain in this dispensation (D&C 77:3).

Man is the child of God, formed in the divine image and endowed with divine attributes, and even as the infant son of an earthly father and mother is capable in due time of becoming a man, so the undeveloped offspring of celestial parentage is capable, by experience through ages and aeons, of evolving into a God.

JOSEPH F. SMITH,
JOHN R. WINDER,
ANTHON H. LUND,
First Presidency of The Church of Jesus Christ of Latter-day Saints
November 1909[64]

WORDS IN SEASON FROM THE FIRST PRESIDENCY
Deseret Evening News, December 17, 1910, part 1, p. 3

In this Christmas message, the First Presidency devoted several sentences to the Church's position with regard to questions raised by science:

Diversity of opinion does not necessitate intolerance of spirit, nor should it embitter or set rational beings against each other. The Christ taught kindness, patience, and charity.

Our religion is not hostile to real science. That which is demonstrated, we accept with joy; but vain philosophy, human theory, and mere speculations of men, we do not accept nor do we adopt anything contrary to divine revelation or to good common sense. But everything that tends to right conduct, that harmonizes with sound morality and increases faith in Deity, finds favor with us no matter where it may be found.

IMPROVEMENT ERA
Vol. XXVIII, SEPTEMBER 1925, No. 11

Editors Table
"Mormon View of Evolution"

A Statement by the First Presidency of
The Church of Jesus Christ of Latter-day Saints.

"God created man in his own image, in the image of God created he him; male and female created he them."

In these plain and pointed words the inspired author of the book of Genesis made known to the world the truth concerning the origin of the human family. Moses, the prophet-historian, who was "learned" we are told, "in all the wisdom of the Egyptians," when making this important announcement, was not voicing a mere opinion. He was speaking as the mouthpiece of God, and his solemn declaration was for all time and for all people. No subsequent revelator of the truth has contradicted the great leader and law-giver of Israel. All who have since spoken by divine authority upon this theme have confirmed his simple and sublime proclamation. Nor could it be otherwise. Truth has but one source, and all revelations from heaven are harmonious one with the other.

Jesus Christ, the Son of God, is "the express image" of his Father's person (Hebrews 1:3). He walked the earth as a human being, as a perfect man, and said, in answer to a question put to him: "He that hath seen me hath seen the Father" (John 14:9). This alone ought to solve the problem to the satisfaction of every thoughtful, reverent mind. It was in this form that the Father and the Son, as two distinct personages, appeared to Joseph Smith, when, as a boy of fourteen years, he received his first vision.

The Father of Jesus Christ is our Father also. Jesus himself taught this truth, when he instructed his disciples how to pray: "Our Father which art in heaven," etc. Jesus, however, is the first born among all the sons of God—the first begotten in the spirit, and the only begotten in the flesh. He is our elder brother, and we, like him, are in the image of God. All men and women are in the similitude of the universal Father and Mother, and are literally sons and daughters of Deity.

Adam, our great progenitor, "the first man," was, like Christ, a premortal spirit, and, like Christ, he took upon him an appropriate body, the body of a man, and so became a "living soul." The doctrine of premortality pours a wonderful flood of light upon the otherwise mysterious problem of man's origin. It shows that man, as a spirit, was begotten and born of heavenly parents, and reared to maturity in the eternal mansions of the Father, prior to coming upon the earth in a temporal body to undergo an experience in mortality.

The Church of Jesus Christ of Latter-day Saints, basing its belief on divine revelation, ancient and modem, proclaims man to be the direct and lineal offspring of Deity. By his Almighty power God organized the earth, and all that it contains, from spirit and element, which exist co-eternally with himself.

Man is the child of God, formed in the divine image and endowed with divine attributes, and even as the infant son of an earthly father and mother is capable in due time of becoming a man, so the undeveloped offspring of celestial parentage is capable, by experience through ages and aeons, of evolving into a God.

HEBER J. GRANT,
ANTHONY W. IVINS,
CHARLES W. NIBLEY,
First Presidency

Encyclopedia of Mormonism

Evolution

The position of the Church on the origin of man was published by the First Presidency in 1909 and stated again by a different First Presidency in 1925:

> "The Church of Jesus Christ of Latter-day Saints, basing its belief on divine revelation, ancient and modern, declares man to be the direct and lineal offspring of Deity. . . . Man is the child of God, formed in the divine image and endowed with divine attributes. . . ."

The scriptures tell why man was created, but they do not tell how, though the Lord has promised that he will tell that when he comes again (D&C 101:32–33). In 1931, when there was intense discussion on the issue of organic evolution, the First Presidency of the Church, then consisting of Presidents Heber J. Grant, Anthony W. Ivins, and Charles W. Nibley, addressed all of the General Authorities of the Church on the matter, and concluded,

> "Upon the fundamental doctrines of the Church we are all agreed. Our mission is to bear the message of the restored gospel to the world. Leave geology, biology, archaeology, and anthropology, no one of which has to do with the salvation of the souls of mankind, to scientific research, while we magnify our calling in the realm of the Church. . . .
>
> "Upon one thing we should all be able to agree, namely, that Presidents Joseph F. Smith, John R. Winder, and Anthon H. Lund were right when they said: "Adam is the primal parent of our race" [First Presidency Minutes, Apr. 7, 1931].[65]

Endnotes

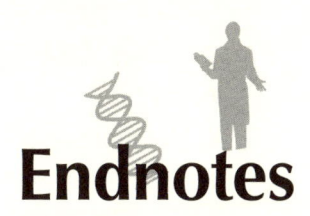

1. F. David Peat, *From Certainty to Uncertainty*, 71.
2. Brigham Young, *Discourses of Brigham Young*, 11.
3. John Grant, *Discarded Science: Ideas that Seemed Good at the Time*, 8.
4. Joseph Smith, *History of the Church,* 2:14; see also *Teachings of Presidents of the Church: Joseph Smith*, 39.
5. Young, *Discourses of Brigham Young*, 2–3, 448; see also *Teachings of Presidents of the Church: Brigham Young*, 16–18.
6. Brigham Young, in *Journal of Discourses,* 14:116.
7. John Taylor, in *Journal of Discourses,* 16:369.
8. Boyd K. Packer, "I Say unto You, Be One," 89.
9. Rodney J. Brown, "A Scientist's View of Life from a 'Mormon' Perspective," 517–19.
10. Bruce R. McConkie, "How to Get Personal Revelation," 8.
11. Brown, "A Scientist's View of Life from a 'Mormon' Perspective," 517–19.
12. Daniel J. Boorstin, *The Seekers: The Story of Man's Continuing Quest to Understand His World*, 21.
13. James Gleick, *Isaac Newton,* 62–63.
14. See Karl R. Popper, *Realism and the Aim of Science;* and Herbert Keuth, *The Philosophy of Karl Popper.*
15. Brown, "A Scientist's View of Life from a 'Mormon' Perspective," 517–19.
16. Albert Einstein, "Science and Religion," 828–35.

17. Richard Feynman, *The Meaning of It All*, 35.
18. In Henry J. Eyring, *Mormon Scientist: The Life and Faith of Henry Eyring*, 246.
19. Francis Collins, *The Language of God: A Scientist Presents Evidence for Belief*, 6.
20. Kenneth R. Miller, *Finding Darwin's God: A Scientist's Search for Common Ground Between God and Evolution*, 267-268.
21. Stephen Hawking, *A Brief History of Time: From the Big Bang to Black Holes*, 175.
22. N. B. Lundwall, *Masterful Discourses and Writings of Orson Pratt*, 13.
23. Ibid., 15.
24. See David L. Clark, *Of Heaven and Earth: Reconciling Scientific Thought with LDS Theology*, 1-225.
25. See John R. Talmage, *The Talmage Story;* and Paul Alan Cox, "Journey to City Creek: Adding Scholarship to Discipleship."
26. See John Andreas Widtsoe, *In a Sunlit Land: The Autobiography of John A. Widtsoe;* and Alan K. Parrish, *John A. Widtsoe: A Biography*.
27. See Henry J. Eyring, *Mormon Scientist: The Life and Faith of Henry Eyring;* Henry Eyring, *The Faith of a Scientist;* and Henry Eyring, *Reflections of a Scientist*.
28. Richard G. Scott, "Truth: The Foundation of Correct Decisions," *Ensign*, November 2007, 90–93.
29. Ezra Taft Benson, "What I Hope You Will Teach Your Children about the Temple," *Ensign*, August 1985, 8.
30. Charles Seife, "What Is the Universe Made Of?" 102.
31. Jack Repchek, *Copernicus' Secret: How the Scientific Revolution Began*, xiii.
32. Lawrence M. Krause and Robert J. Scherrer, "The End of Cosmology?" Scientific American, March 2008, 46.
33. Smith, *History of the Church*, 3:385–91.
34. "Evolution," in *Encyclopedia of Mormonism*, 2:478.

35. Ibid.
36. National Academy of Sciences and Institute of Medicine, *Science, Evolution, and Creationism*, 4.
37. Eugenie Carol Scott, *Evolution vs. Creationism: An Introduction*.
38. Smith, *History of the Church*, 4:554–55.
39. "The Genetic Tree of Life: Some Assembly Required," *BYU BioAg Magazine* (Fall 2005): 8–9.
40. Eyring, *Mormon Scientist*, 5.
41. Kristi L. Bowman, "The evolution battles in high-school science classes: Who is teaching what?" 6:69–74.
42. National Academy of Sciences and Institute of Medicine, *Science, Evolution, and Creationism*, 37.
43. Scott, *Evolution vs. Creationism: An Introduction*, 211.
44. Bowman, "The evolution battles in high-school science classes: Who is teaching what?" 6:69–74.
45. Scott, *Evolution vs. Creationism: An Introduction*, 116-117.
46. National Academy of Sciences and Institute of Medicine, *Science, Evolution, and Creationism*, 40.
47. R. J. Brown, "Green Revolution to Gene Revolution," 4–5.
48. Antony Trewavas, "Malthus foiled again and again," *Nature* 418 (August 8, 2002): 668–70.
49. *Feeding the World*, 7-8.
50. "Borlaug's Revolution," *Wall Street Journal*, July 17, 2007, A16.
51. National Agricultural Statistics Service.
52. Jared Diamond, *Collapse: How Societies Choose to Fail or Succeed*, 494-496.
53. Erik Stokstad, "Will Malthus Continue to Be Wrong?" 102.
54. John E. Dowling, *The Great Brain Debate: Nature or Nurture?* 7.
55. Daniel G. Gibson, Gwynedd A. Benders, Cynthia Andrews-Pfannkoch, et. al. "Complete Chemical Synthesis, Assembly, and Cloning of *Mycoplasma genitalium* Genome," 1215–20.

56. Grant, 8.
57. Repchek, 8–9.
58. Gleick, 185–86.
59. Maitland Jones Jr., *Organic Chemistry*, 1.
60. Ibid., 1–2.
61. Timothy Ferris, ed., *The World Treasury of Physics, Astronomy, and Mathematics*, 3–145.
62. Boorstin, *The Discoverers: A History of Man's Search to Know His World and Himself*, 430.
63. Alexander Hellemans and Bryan Bunch, *The Timetables of Science: A Chronology of the Most Important People and Events in the History of Science*, 278.
64. Reprinted in the *Ensign*, February 2002, 26–30; punctuation, paragraphing, and spelling are standardized.
65. "Evolution," in *Encyclopedia of Mormonism*, 2:478.

Bibliography

Benson, Ezra Taft. "What I Hope You Will Teach Your Children about the Temple," *Ensign*, August 1985, 8.

Boorstin, Daniel J. *The Discoverers: A History of Man's Search to Know His World and Himself.* New York: Random House, 1983.

_____. *The Seekers: The Story of Man's Continuing Quest to Understand His World.* New York: Random House, 1998.

"Borlaug's Revolution." *Wall Street Journal,* July 17, 2007, A16.

Bowman, Kristi L. "The evolution battles in high-school science classes: who is teaching what?" *Front Ecol Environ* 6 (March 2008): 69–74.

Brown, R. J. "Green Revolution to Gene Revolution," *Life Sciences,* Fall 2007, 4–5.

Brown, Rodney J. "A Scientist's View of Life from a 'Mormon' Perspective." In Gyula Palyi, Claudia Zucchi, and Luciano Caglioti. *Fundamentals of Life.* New York: Elsevier, 2002.

Clark, David L., ed. *Of Heaven and Earth: Reconciling Scientific Thought with LDS Theology.* Salt Lake City: Deseret Book, 1988.

Collins, Francis. *The Language of God: A Scientist Presents Evidence for Belief.* New York: Free Press, 2006.

Cox, Paul Alan. "Journey to City Creek: Adding Scholarship to Discipleship." In *On Becoming a Disciple-Scholar.* Edited by Henry B. Eyring. Salt Lake City: Bookcraft, 1995.

Diamond, Jared. *Collapse: How Societies Choose to Fail or Succeed.* New York: Penguin Books, 2005.

Dowling, John E. *The Great Brain Debate: Nature or Nurture?* Washington, D.C.: Joseph Henry Press, 2004.

Einstein, Albert. "Science and Religion." In *The World Treasury of Physics, Astronomy, and Mathematics.* Edited by Timothy Ferris. New York: Little, Brown and Company, 1991, 828–35.

Encyclopedia of Mormonism. Edited by Daniel H. Ludlow. 5 vols. New York: Macmillan, 1992.

Eyring, Henry. *The Faith of a Scientist.* Salt Lake City: Bookcraft, 1969.

Eyring, Henry. *Reflections of a Scientist.* Salt Lake City: Deseret Book, 1983.

Eyring, Henry B. ed. *On Becoming a Disciple-Scholar.* Salt Lake City: Bookcraft, 1995.

Eyring, Henry J. *Mormon Scientist: The Life and Faith of Henry Eyring.* Salt Lake City: Deseret Book, 2007.

Feeding the World. Washington, D.C.: Pew Initiative on Food and Biotechnology, 2004.

Ferris, Timothy, ed. *The World Treasury of Physics, Astronomy, and Mathematics.* New York: Little, Brown and Company, 1991.

Feynman, Richard. *The Meaning of It All.* Reading, Mass.: Perseus Books, 1998.

Gibson, Daniel G., Gwynedd A. Benders, Cynthia Andrews-Pfannkoch, et al. "Complete Chemical Synthesis, Assembly, and Cloning of *Mycoplasma genitalium* Genome," *Science* 319 (February 29, 2008): 1215–20.

Gleick, James. *Isaac Newton.* New York: Pantheon Books, 2003.

Grant, John. *Discarded Science: Ideas that Seemed Good at the Time.* London: Facts, Figures & Fun, 2006.

Hawking, Stephen. *A Brief History of Time: From the Big Bang to Black Holes.* New York: Bantam Books, 1988.

Hellemans, Alexander, and Bryan Bunch. *The Timetables of Science: A Chronology of the Most Important People and Events in the History of Science.* New York: Simon and Schuster, 1991.

Jones, Maitland, Jr. *Organic Chemistry.* 3rd ed. New York: W. W. Norton & Company, Inc., 2003.

Journal of Discourses. 26 vols. London: Latter-day Saints' Book Depot, 1854–86.

Keuth, Herbert. *The Philosophy of Karl Popper.* Cambridge: Cambridge University Press, 2004.

Krause, Lawrence M. and Robert J. Scherrer. The End of Cosmology?" *Scientific American,* March 2008, **46**.

Lundwall, N. B. *Masterful Discourses and Writings of Orson Pratt.* Salt Lake City: N. B. Lundwall, 1953.

McConkie, Bruce R. *How to Get Personal Revelation.* Brigham Young University Speeches of the Year. October 11, 1966.

Miller, Kenneth R. *Finding Darwin's God: A Scientist's Search for Common Ground Between God and Evolution.* New York: Harper, 1999.

National Academy of Sciences and Institute of Medicine. *Science, Evolution, and Creationism.* Washington, D.C.: The National Academies Press, 2008.

National Agricultural Statistics Service. U.S. Department of Agriculture, 2007; see http://www.nass.usda.gov/Newsroom/2007/06_29_2007.asp

Packer, Boyd K. " 'I Say unto You, Be One.' " In *Brigham Young University 1990–91 Devotional and Fireside Speeches.* Provo, Utah: Brigham Young University, 1991, 81–91.

Parrish, Alan K. *John A. Widtsoe: a Biography.* Salt Lake City: Deseret Book, 2003.

Peat, F. David. *From Certainty to Uncertainty.* Washington, D.C.: Joseph Henry Press, 2002.

Popper, Karl R. *Realism and the Aim of Science.* London: Hutchinson & Co., 1983.

Repchek, Jack. *Copernicus' Secret: How the Scientific Revolution Began.* New York: Simon & Schuster, 2007.

Scott, Eugenie Carol. *Evolution vs. Creationism: An Introduction.* Berkley, Calif.: University of California Press, 2005.

Scott, Richard G. "Truth: The Foundation of Correct Decisions," *Ensign,* November 2007, 90–93.

Seife, Charles. "What Is the Universe Made Of?" *Science* 309 (July 1, 2005): 102.

Smith, Joseph. *History of The Church of Jesus Christ of Latter-day Saints.* Edited by B. H. Roberts. 2nd ed. rev., 7 vols. Salt Lake City: The Church of Jesus Christ of Latter-day Saints, 1932–51.

_____. *Teachings of Presidents of the Church: Joseph Smith.* Salt Lake City: The Church of Jesus Christ of Latter-day Saints, 2007.

Stokstad, Erik. "Will Malthus Continue to Be Wrong?" *Science* 309 (July 2005): 102.

Talmage, John R. *The Talmage Story.* Salt Lake City: Bookcraft, 1972.

"The Genetic Tree of Life: Some Assembly Required," *BYU BioAg Magazine* (Fall 2005): 8–9.

Trewavas, Antony. "Malthus foiled again and again," *Nature* 418 (August 8, 2002): 668–70.

Widtsoe, John A. *In a Sunlit Land: The Autobiography of John A. Widtsoe.* Salt Lake City: Deseret News, 1952.

Young, Brigham. *Discourses of Brigham Young.* Selected by John A. Widtsoe. Salt Lake City: Deseret Book, 1954.

_____. *Teachings of Presidents of the Church: Brigham Young.* Salt Lake City: The Church of Jesus Christ of Latter-day Saints, 1997.

Author Biographical Information

Dr. Rodney J. Brown was raised in Coalville, Utah, as a member of The Church of Jesus Christ of Latter-day Saints. He served a mission as a young man in Alaska and British Columbia and has served in a variety of callings since then.

He graduated from Brigham Young University (B.S.), Utah State University (M.S.), and North Carolina State University (Ph.D.) and spent two years as a research scientist at Weizmann Institute of Science in Israel. Since then, he is now employed as the Dean of the College of Biology and Agriculture at Brigham Young University. Before going to BYU in 2005, he was Deputy Under Secretary of Agriculture in Washington, DC.

He and his wife, Sandra, have three children and eleven grandchildren.

SETTING THE RECORD STRAIGHT SERIES

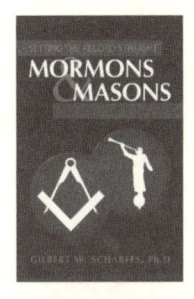

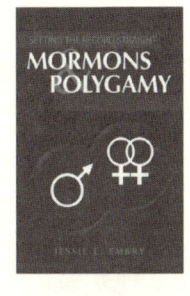

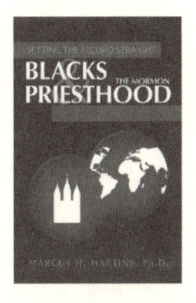

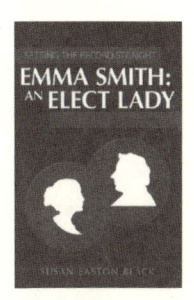

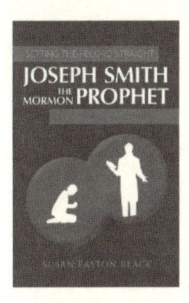

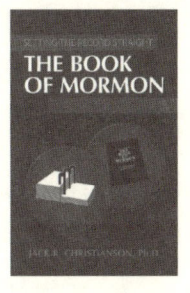

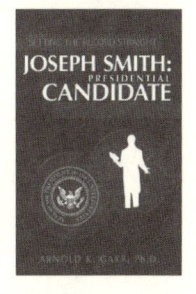

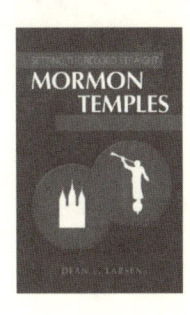

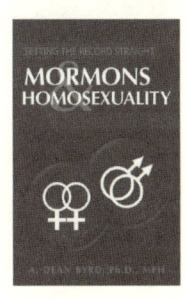

- MORMONS & MASONS — Gilbert W. Scharffs, Ph.D.
- MORMONS & POLYGAMY — Jessie L. Embry
- BLACKS & THE MORMON PRIESTHOOD — Marcus H. Martins, Ph.D.
- EMMA SMITH: AN ELECT LADY — Susan Easton Black
- JOSEPH SMITH THE MORMON PROPHET — Susan Easton Black
- THE BOOK OF MORMON — Jack R. Christianson, Ph.D.
- THE WORD OF WISDOM — Steven C. Harper, Ph.D.
- JOSEPH SMITH: PRESIDENTIAL CANDIDATE — Arnold K. Garr, Ph.D.
- MORMON TEMPLES — Dean L. Larsen
- MORMONS & HOMOSEXUALITY — A. Dean Byrd, Ph.D., MPH
- MORMONS & SCIENCE — Rodney J. Brown, Ph.D.
- MORMON FUNDAMENTALISM — Brian C. Hales

To learn more about these and other Millennial Press titles, visit www.millennialpress.com. Available wherever books are sold.